Our Planet Needs Us!

Record cold winters. Heat waves. Droughts and floods and cyclones. Have you noticed how erratic the climate has become in the last few years? Some places are receiving unseasonal rainfall in extreme doses (which causes floods), while other places are receiving no rainfall even when it's expected! Why does it happen, you might ask? Well, because of Climate Change – that's when Mother Nature goes to extremes. How? Let's find out!

Hot Blanket

Earth is surrounded by a blanket of gases which lets the heat in and traps it close to the earth's surface, which is good. For we can't live without warmth!

What's Happening Now?

Factories, cars, etc. are belching out too much of one of these gases called carbon-dioxide.

What Does it Change?

Scientists believe that the excess of carbon-dioxide is changing the climate, because the 'blanket' is holding too much of heat. This is called Global Warming.

What Can Happen?

If Earth's temperature continues to get hotter, polar ice will start melting; raising the ocean levels and wiping out islands!

What Will Change Then?

When the oceans warm up, sea life can die. There can be more floods. Also, the places that grow most of the food can get too warm to grow crops.

How Can We Help?

We have to do something! And each one of us can help – by using less energy, protecting and planting trees, and recycling used goods!

Ladakh!

Photographs by
Nandakumar Narasimhan

Deserts are hot and dry. So can a desert be cold?

Well, Ladakh is! It is one of the coldest deserts in the world!

Ladakh is in the state of Jammu and Kashmir. It is more than 9,800 feet above sea level. Want to know how high that is? If you can, put 245 three-storeyed flats one on top of another! Now climb all the way up and stand on top of it! You'll be standing in a place as high as Ladakh.

Some people who live in Ladakh are known as Changpas or Drukpas. They are wandering shepherds. Each Changpa family owns a flock of 100 to 300 sheep. They do not live in the same place for a whole year, and go wherever the grass is green, for their animals.

Life goes on in the highlands of
Changthang Plateau in western Ladakh,
no matter how the weather is. The
Changpas grow barley, wheat and peas.
They keep yak, cows and dzos.

Ladakh has many glaciers. They are important for all of us. But because of increase in pollution and cutting down of trees, Earth is becoming warmer and the glaciers in Ladakh are melting. How do you think you can help?

beach blues

By Libby Hathorn
Art by Tasneem Amiruddin

We walked this beach once

Among shells and driftwood

Before the road came,

Climbed the secret dampish rocks,

Trailed through laden sea pools,

Steaming afternoons,

In salty shafts of sunlight.

Now sixty-six new buildings,

High and mighty buildings,

Cloud the sky

And rob the beach of sun

From midday on,

And sixty-six thousand people

Have taken all the shells.

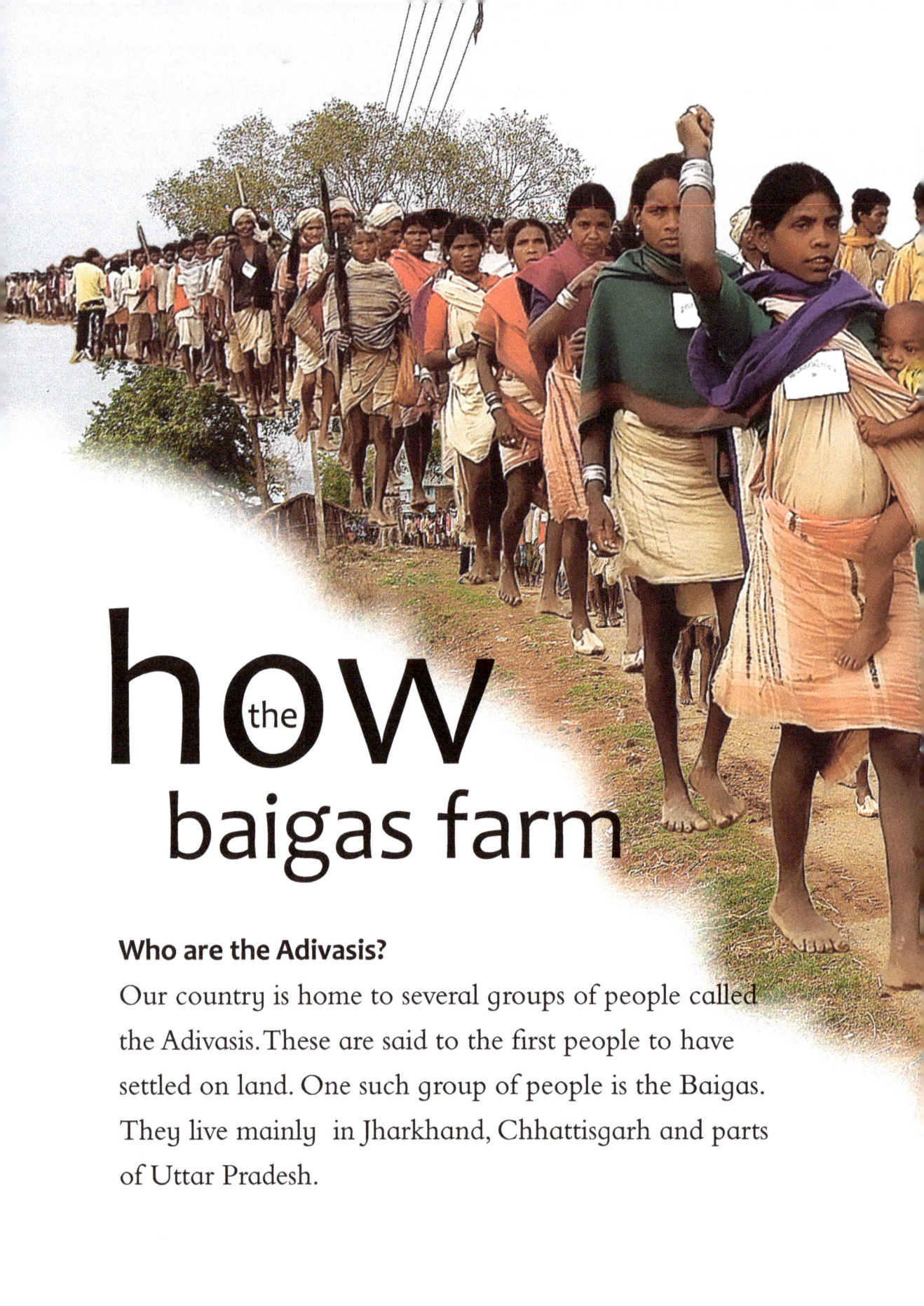

how
the
baigas farm

Who are the Adivasis?

Our country is home to several groups of people called
the Adivasis. These are said to the first people to have
settled on land. One such group of people is the Baigas.
They live mainly in Jharkhand, Chhattisgarh and parts
of Uttar Pradesh.

The Baigas

Like all Adivasi people, the Baigas are a peace-loving community. Originally, Baigas lived in forests. They believe that God of Tree has created them and it's their duty to protect the forests.

Sowing the Seeds of Change

The Baigas practise a unique form of agriculture called 'Shifting Cultivation'. They select a patch of land and clear it of fallen leaves. They then burn the leaves and scatter the ash on their patch to make the soil fertile.

Tackling Climate Change

But now, global warming has affected climate patterns all over the world. We are faced with extreme forms of weather. And the Baigas have given us a unique agricultural solution! If one crop fails due to some reason, the other crops can help the farmers survive!

Back to the Roots!

The Baigas, like all Adivasi people, understand nature and its ways very well. They can provide us with new ideas about how to use resources in a sustainable and eco-friendly manner.

Let us all give the knowledge of our Adivasi friends a chance!

Photographs: Wikimedia Commons

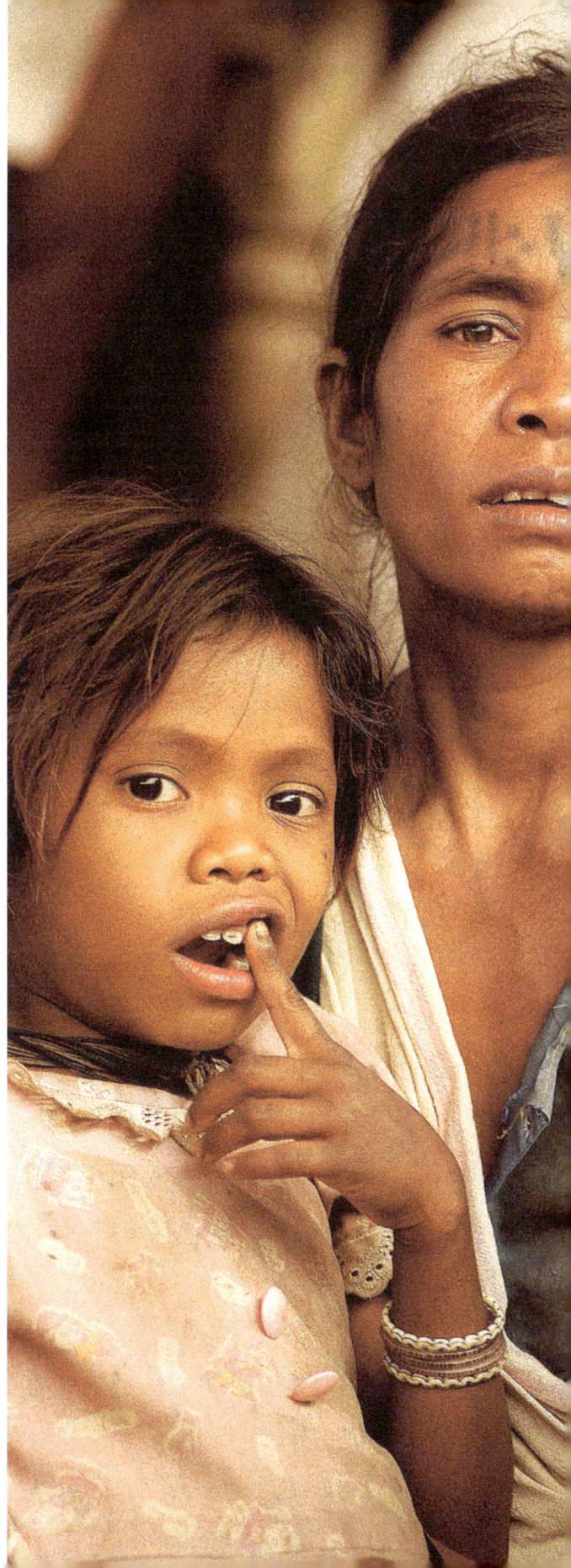

the cracked pitcher

By Paulo Coelho
Translated from the Portuguese
by Margaret Jull Costa
Art by Vincent van Gogh *(Garden at Arles, 1888)*

Once there lived a man who used to carry water every day to his village, using two large pitchers tied on either end of a piece of wood, which he placed across his shoulders.

One of the pitchers was older than the other and was full of small cracks. Every time the man came back along the path to his house, half of the water was lost. For two years, the man made the same journey. The younger pitcher was always very proud of the way it did its work and was sure that it was up to the task for which it had been created. The other pitcher was mortally ashamed that it could carry out only half its task, even though it knew that the cracks were the result of long years of work.

So ashamed was the old pitcher that, one day, while the man was preparing to fill it up with water from the well, it decided to speak to him. "I wish to apologize because, due to my age, you only manage to take home half the water you fill me with, and thus quench only half the thirst awaiting you in your house."

The man smiled and said, "When we go back, be sure to take a careful look at the path."

The pitcher did as the man asked and noticed many flowers and plants growing along one side of the path.

"Do you see how much more beautiful nature is on your side of the road?" the man remarked. "I knew you had cracks, but I decided to take advantage of them. I sowed vegetables and flowers there, and you always watered them. I've picked dozens of roses to decorate my house, and my children have had lettuce, cabbage and onions to eat. If you were not the way you are, I could never have done this. We all, at some point, grow old and acquire other qualities which can always be turned to good advantage."

Home to creatures big and small,

to the wind and waterfall,

to the trees and all things green,

to the worm that works unseen.

Earthsong

By Geeta Dharmarajan

Art by Aparna Bhandar

To elephants that roam the wild,

to cows and draft animals mild,

to men and women, children, too

our earth's a gift in green and blue.

Let's enjoy this planet rare

Let's remember to care and share.

Landscape

By Kamala Das
Art by Rekha Krishnan

This summer day
heaps red dust on the road
meandering across the treeless hill.

Tyres of cars, buses, trucks and jeeps
and the chimneys of the steel plant
belch red dust all the time.

How then can the gulmohur
preserve its own redness?

GREEN
HOPE

In a world dealing with Climate Change, one girl found herself more than ready to create her own organization to tackle the problem. Kehkashan Basu was twelve when she founded Green Hope—an organization which works for protecting our environment, planting trees and spreading awareness about Climate Change. Green Hope currently has more than 1000 members.

Known as "eco warrior" and winner of 2016 Children's Peace Prize, Basu is also the youngest person to be chosen as UNEP's (United Nations Environment Programme) Global Coordinator for Children & Youth. Settled in the UAE, Basu is of Indian heritage. Her organization is based in over ten countries.

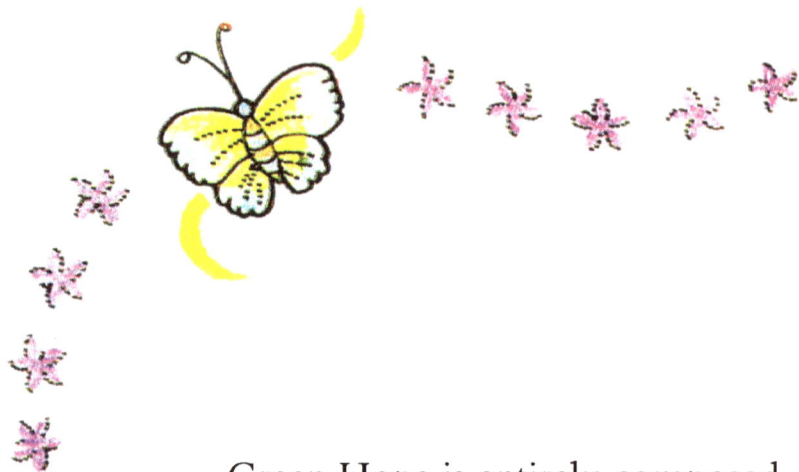

Green Hope is entirely composed of children. It is even funded by children! Children who work in Green Hope use their pocket money to fund their activities.

Kehkashan is an example to all of us who wish to work towards a better world. One does not need wealth or age to make a difference. It is the desire to do good which will lead us to everything we require in time. Her proactive attitude is reflected in her words when she says she believes in taking actions 'within her zone of influence and not depend on others'.

THEME TALK

Let's Change Climate Change

For life to sustain on Earth, it is very important to have balance. For instance, we cannot live without the right amount of heat and warmth but an excess of the same has caused Global Warming. How do you think we can maintain this balance?

Discover, Learn, Create and Innovate

Sonam Wangchuk, an innovative engineer from Ladakh, thought up a unique idea to tackle the problem of disappearing glaciers — by making artificial glaciers in the form of 'ice-stupas'! Find out more about Sonam.

Eco-friendly Living

A lot of our forests and natural spaces are cleared off to construct more roads and buildings. There can be several ill-effects of this. Explore ways through which we can live sustainably, without harming our environment.

Adivasis Look Towards a Better Tomorrow

An Adivasi is where the jungle is… goes an old saying. Through centuries, Adivasis have enjoyed a close bond with nature. They never try to harm nature, but become a part of it. Create awareness about India's Adivasi communities! Dedicate each month to an Adivasi community and discover about their language, culture, arts, etc.

Be a Green Activist!

Start a kitchen garden in your school or neighbourhood. Take help from teachers/elders. Take turns with your friends in buying seeds, fertilisers and other requirements. Monitor how the seeds germinate and begin to bear fruits.

Care and Share

Discuss with your friends about how to use resources and energy responsibly. Prepare a list of things we can do and share it with your family and neighbours.

Traffic Jams

Traffic jams are so common in our city streets these days. More cars mean we need more roads; more roads mean that we have to cut stretches of hills and trees to expand the space of the city. Do you think this is sustainable?

List a few ways in which we can lessen the usage of private vehicles.

Save the Planet

Can we think of ways to conserve resources in our daily life? Listed below are some things to start you off:

- Buy less.
- Do not waste food.
- Turn the tap off when brushing teeth, when soaping your hands or scrubbing utensils.
- Use a bucket of water to bathe instead of the shower.
- Find ways to store rainwater.
- Use public transport. Walk or cycle, whenever possible.

Our Contributors

Aparna Bhandar is a folk painter who specializes in Warli, Madhubani, Egyptian, Gond, Tanjore, Pattachitra, and Mandana paintings. **| Geeta Dharmarajan** loves writing for children. She received the Padma Shri in 2012 for her work in literature & education. **| Kamala Das** was an Indian English poet and a leading Malayalam author from Kerala. **| Libby Hathorn** is an award-winning Australian poet and the author of more than fifty books. **| Margaret Jull Costa** is a British translator of Portuguese and Spanish literature. **| Nandakumar Narasimhan** is a photographer based in Singapore. He loves to talk to people and capture them through his lens. **| Paulo Coelho** is a Brazilian author who has dedicated his life completely to literature. **| Rekha Krishnan** is a renowned artist who has been exhibiting her paintings in India and internationally for more than thirty years. **| Tasneem Amiruddin** is an illustrator from Mumbai who's inspired by gorgeous sunsets and mischievous children. **| Vincent Willem van Gogh** was a Dutch painter. He used expressive and spontaneous colours in his paintings.

KATHA

First published by Katha, 2076
Copyright © Katha, 2017
Text copyright © Katha, 2017
Illustrations copyright © respective artists, 2017
All rights reserved. No part of this book may be reproduced or utilized in any form without the prior written permission of the publisher.
ISBN 978-93-82454-80-9
E-mail: marketing@katha.org, Website: www.katha.org

KATHA is a registered nonprofit organization started in 1988. We work in the literacy to literature continuum. Devoted to enhancing the joys of reading amongst children and adults, we work with more than 1,00,000 children in poverty, to bring them to grade-level reading through quality books and interventions.
A3, Sarvodaya Enclave, Sri Aurobindo Marg, New Delhi 110 017
Phone: 4141 6600 . 4182 9998 . 2652 1752 . Fax: 2651 4373

All stories are by Geeta Dharmarajan, except where specifically stated. © Geeta Dharmarajan, 2017.

Ten per cent of sales proceeds from this book will support the quality education of children studying in Katha Schools.
Katha regularly plants trees to replace the wood used in the making of its books.

VISION PARTNER: ASHOKA INNOVATORS FOR THE PUBLIC

Ashoka envisions a world in which every young person grows up to become a changemaker — a world in which the development of changemakers and the practice of changemaking are the norm — a world in which everyone knows they can change the world for the better, and does so.

ORACLE GIVING

Advancing education, protecting the environment, enriching community life ... and inspiring changemaking in children.

KATHA, a non-profit organization, works in the literacy to literature continuum. We work with poor urban and rural communities, with governments and municipal corporation schools to ensure that every child learns to read for fun and at grade level.

www.ingramcontent.com/pod-product-compliance
Lightning Source LLC
Chambersburg PA
CBHW041634040426
42447CB00020B/3489